You Can Draw

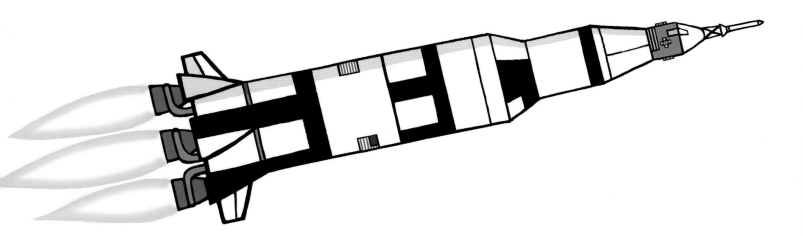

Rockets

 **Gareth Stevens**
Publishing

Please visit our website, **www.garethstevens.com**.
For a free color catalog of all our high-quality books,
call toll free 1-800-542-2595 or fax 1-877-542-2596.

Library of Congress Cataloging-in-Publication Data

Bergin, Mark, 1961-
Rockets / Mark Bergin.
     pages cm - (You can draw)
Includes index.
ISBN 978-1-4339-7475-5 (pbk.)
ISBN 978-1-4339-7476-2 (6-pack)
ISBN 978-1-4339-7474-8 (library binding)
1. Rocketry in art-Juvenile literature.
2. Space ships in art-Juvenile literature.
3. Drawing-Technique-Juvenile literature. I. Title.
NC825.R6B47 2012
743'.8962947-dc23
                              2011052969

First Edition

Published in 2013 by
Gareth Stevens Publishing
111 East 14th Street, Suite 349
New York, NY 10003

© 2013 The Salariya Book Company Ltd

Editor: Rob Walker

Printed in China

CPSIA compliance information: Batch #SS12GS: For further information contact Gareth Stevens,
New York, New York at 1-800-542-2595.

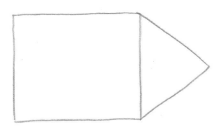

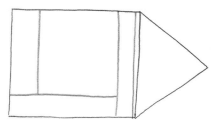

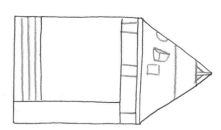

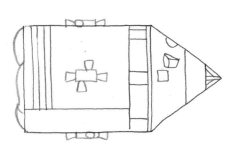

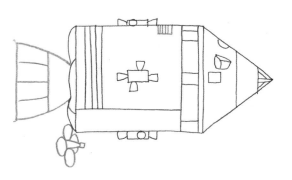

You Can Draw

Rockets

By Mark Bergin

Contents

6   Introduction

8   Materials

10 Inspiration

12 Mercury-Redstone

14 Saturn V

16 Apollo CSM

18 X-2

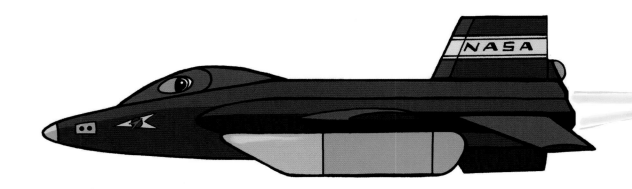

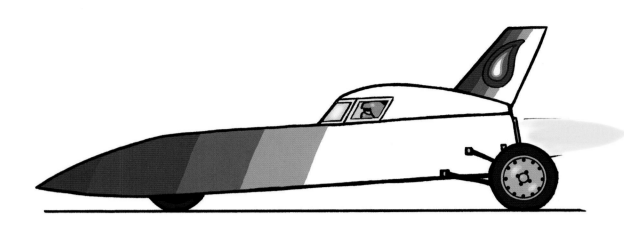

20 Blue Flame

22 Space shuttle

24 X-15

26 Ariane

28 SpaceShipOne

30 More views

32 Glossary and Index

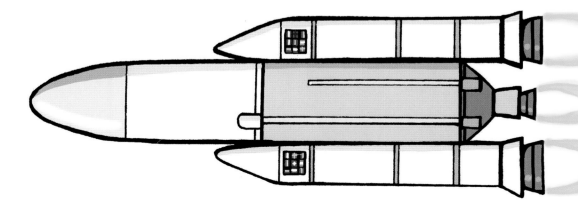

Introduction

Learning to draw is fun. In this book, a finished drawing will be broken up into stages as a guide to completing your own drawing. However, this is only the beginning. The more you practice, the better you will get. Have fun coming up with cool designs, adding more incredible details, and using new materials to achieve different effects!

This is an example showing how each drawing will be built up in easy stages. New sections of the drawing will be shown in color to make each additional step clear.

1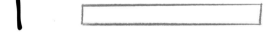

2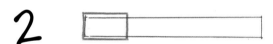

3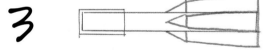

4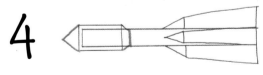

5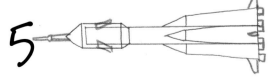

With practice, you too will be able to draw rockets just like the examples shown here.

Materials

There are many different art materials available that you can use to draw and color your vehicles. Try out each one for new and exciting results. The more you practice with them, the better your drawing skills will get!

Use a pencil to draw the shape of your rocket. Any mistakes you make can easily be erased, as can any construction lines that are left over at the end of your drawing.

An eraser can be used to rub out any pencil mistakes. It can also be used to create highlights on pencil drawings.

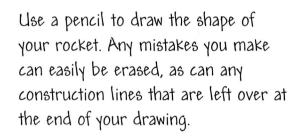

You can go over your finished pencil lines with pen to make the lines bolder. But remember, a pen line is permanent, so you can't erase any mistakes!

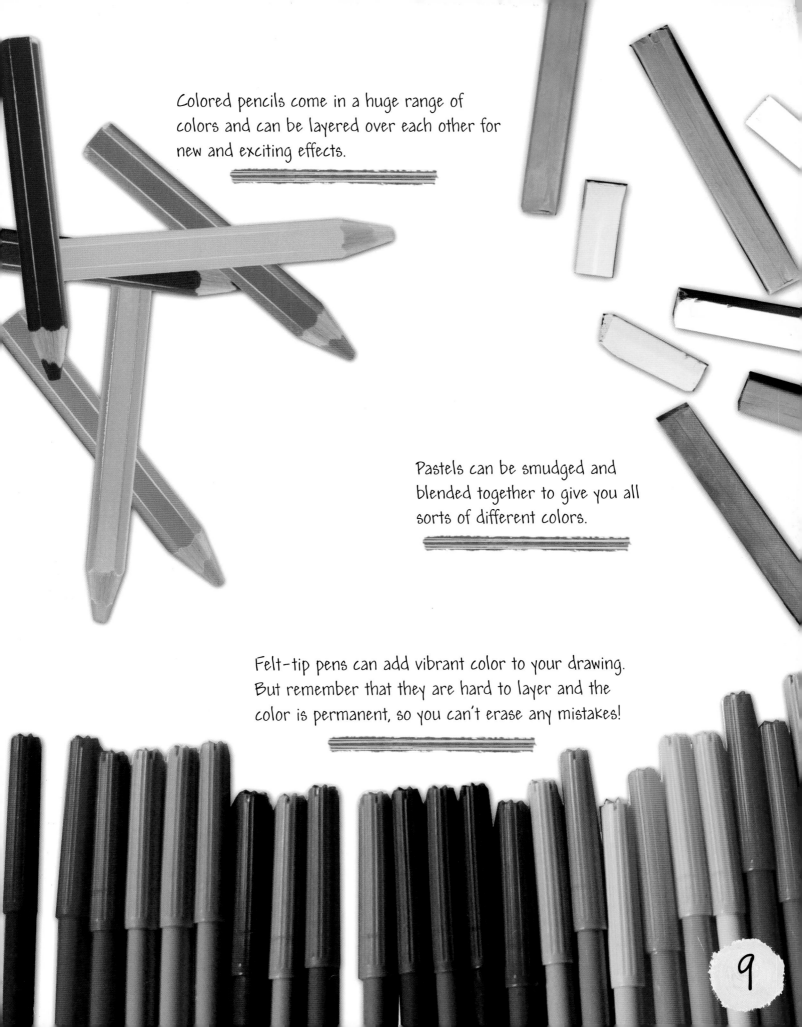

Colored pencils come in a huge range of colors and can be layered over each other for new and exciting effects.

Pastels can be smudged and blended together to give you all sorts of different colors.

Felt-tip pens can add vibrant color to your drawing. But remember that they are hard to layer and the color is permanent, so you can't erase any mistakes!

Inspiration

Many types of rockets are made throughout the world. You can choose any of them as the inspiration for your cartoon-style drawing. Looking at photos, magazines, or books can give you new ideas and new designs to try.

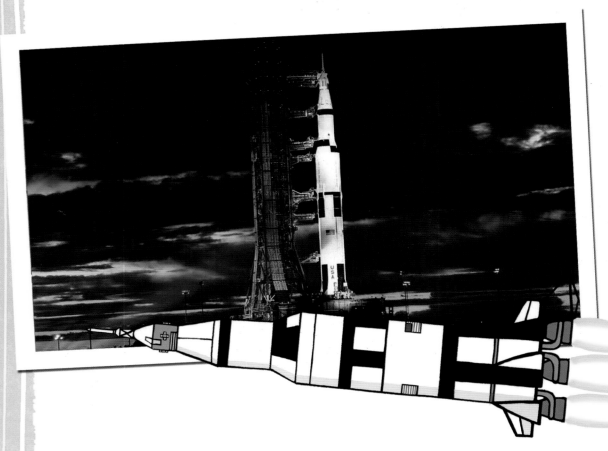

When turning your rocket into a cartoon-style, two-dimensional drawing, concentrate on the key elements you want to include and the overall shape of the rocket.

One way to make your rocket look cool is to exaggerate its key features and perhaps add new ones!

Use different colors and designs to make your rocket look the way you want it to. It's your creation, after all.

Mercury-Redstone

The Mercury-Redstone was a rocket in NASA's Mercury program. It achieved suborbital flight in the 1960s.

Draw a tall rectangle for the main body of the Redstone rocket and divide it into three sections (as shown).

Add more dividing lines and draw a rectangle overlapping the base.

Draw lines to connect the rectangle to the main body. Add fins.

Fins

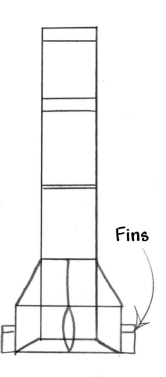

Mercury spacecraft

Draw the Mercury spacecraft on top of the Redstone rocket. Add the rocket nozzles to the base of the rocket.

Nozzles

Escape tower

Add more detail to the Mercury spacecraft and draw the escape tower. Add lines to the top section of the rocket.

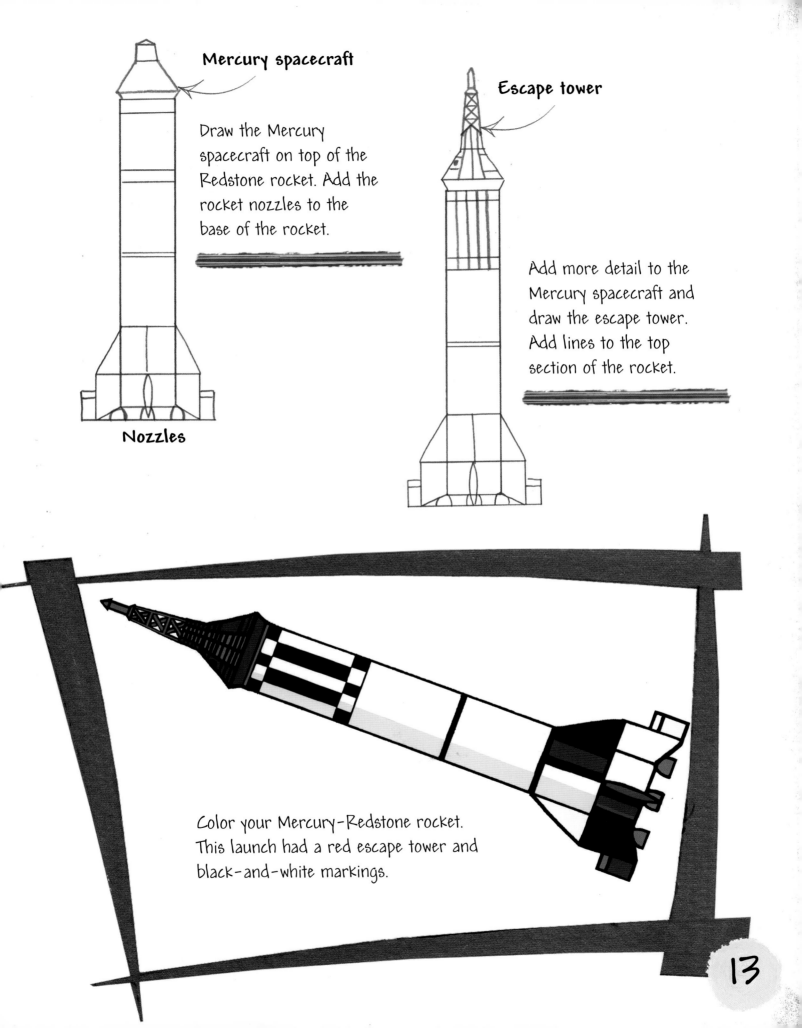

Color your Mercury-Redstone rocket. This launch had a red escape tower and black-and-white markings.

Saturn V

Saturn V is the largest rocket ever operated and was used by NASA for manned spaceflights.

Draw a tall rectangle for the main body of the rocket. Divide it into four sections.

Add detail to each of the main rocket sections.

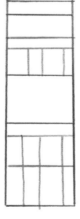

Draw the top section of the rocket.

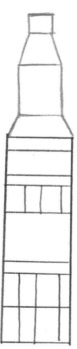

Draw the nose of the rocket's command module. Add fairings and fins to the base of the main rocket section.

Fin

Fairings

Draw the escape tower and add detail to the command module. Add the rocket nozzles and large jets of flame coming out of them.

Complete your drawing by finishing off all the remaining details, then add color.

Apollo CSM

The Apollo CSM (command/service module) could carry three crew members. It was used to reach the moon.

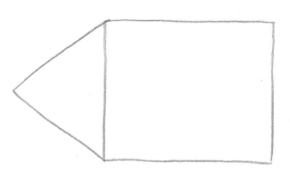

Draw a large box shape for the main body of the CSM and add a pointed nose section.

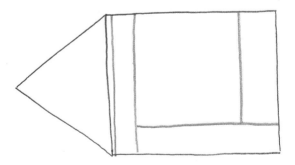

Divide the main body into sections as shown.

Add more details to the nose section and to the main body.

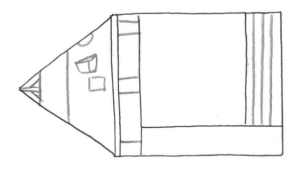

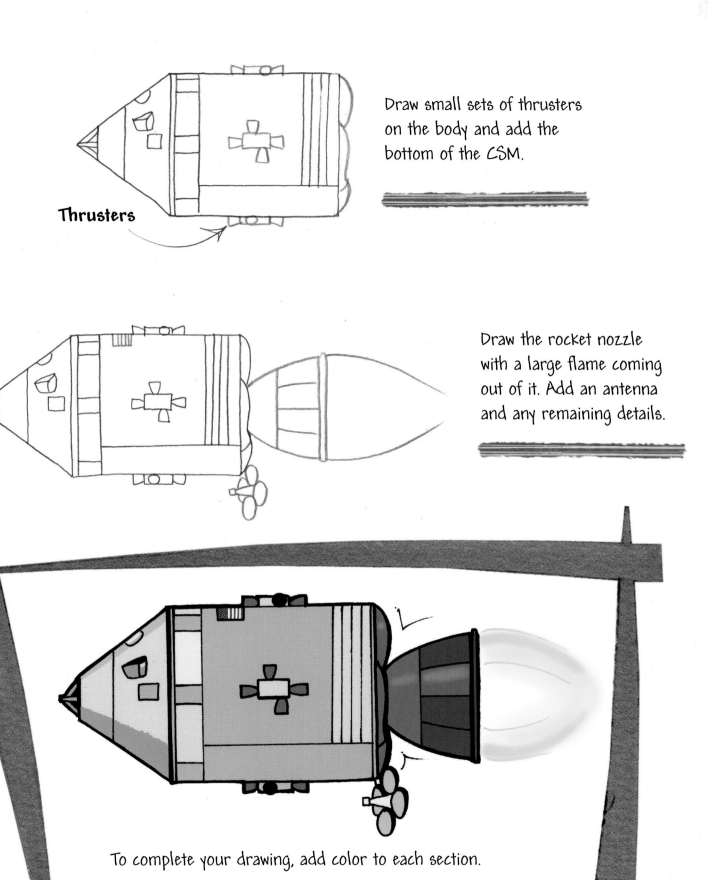

Draw small sets of thrusters on the body and add the bottom of the CSM.

Thrusters

Draw the rocket nozzle with a large flame coming out of it. Add an antenna and any remaining details.

To complete your drawing, add color to each section.

X-2

The Bell X-2 was an experimental aircraft that flew at supersonic speeds using a special rocket engine.

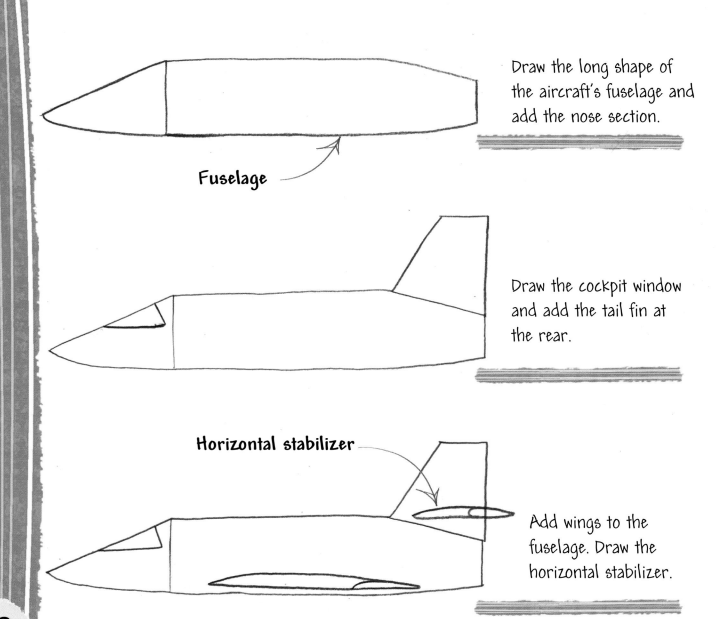

Fuselage

Draw the long shape of the aircraft's fuselage and add the nose section.

Draw the cockpit window and add the tail fin at the rear.

Horizontal stabilizer

Add wings to the fuselage. Draw the horizontal stabilizer.

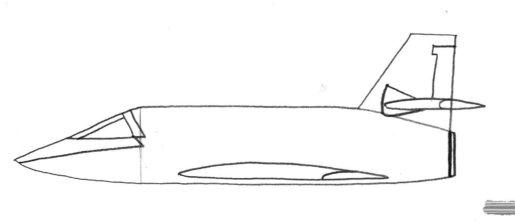

Add more detail to
the cockpit window
and to the tail fin.

Draw the pilot and a
nose spike, and add the
final details to the X-2.

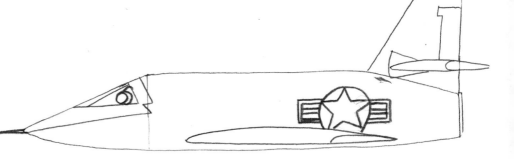

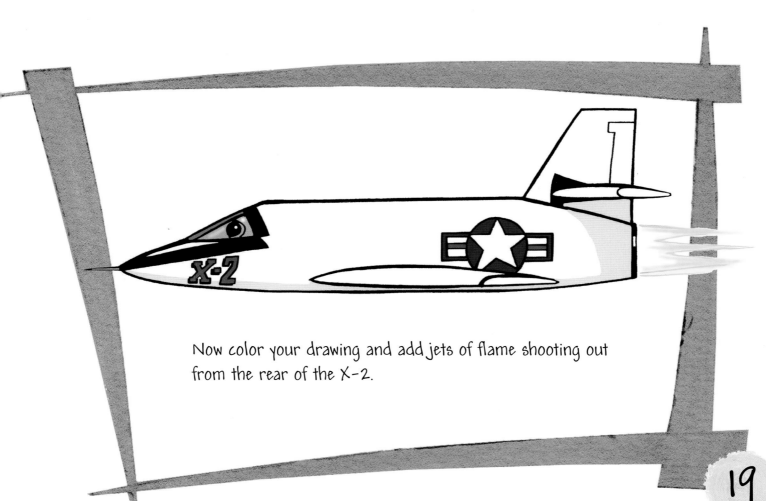

Now color your drawing and add jets of flame shooting out
from the rear of the X-2.

Blue Flame

The Blue Flame was a rocket-powered vehicle that held the land speed record for 13 years. It reached 630.388 mph (1,014.513 kph) in 1970.

Start by drawing the long bullet-shaped body (keep the rear end slightly raised). Add a line for the ground.

Draw the wheels. The front wheel is partially hidden.

Stabilizers

Draw the rear-wheel stabilizers and add detail to each wheel.

Draw the cockpit shape and add a window and the driver's head.

Cockpit

Draw the paintwork design and add a fin and a jet of flame at the rear.

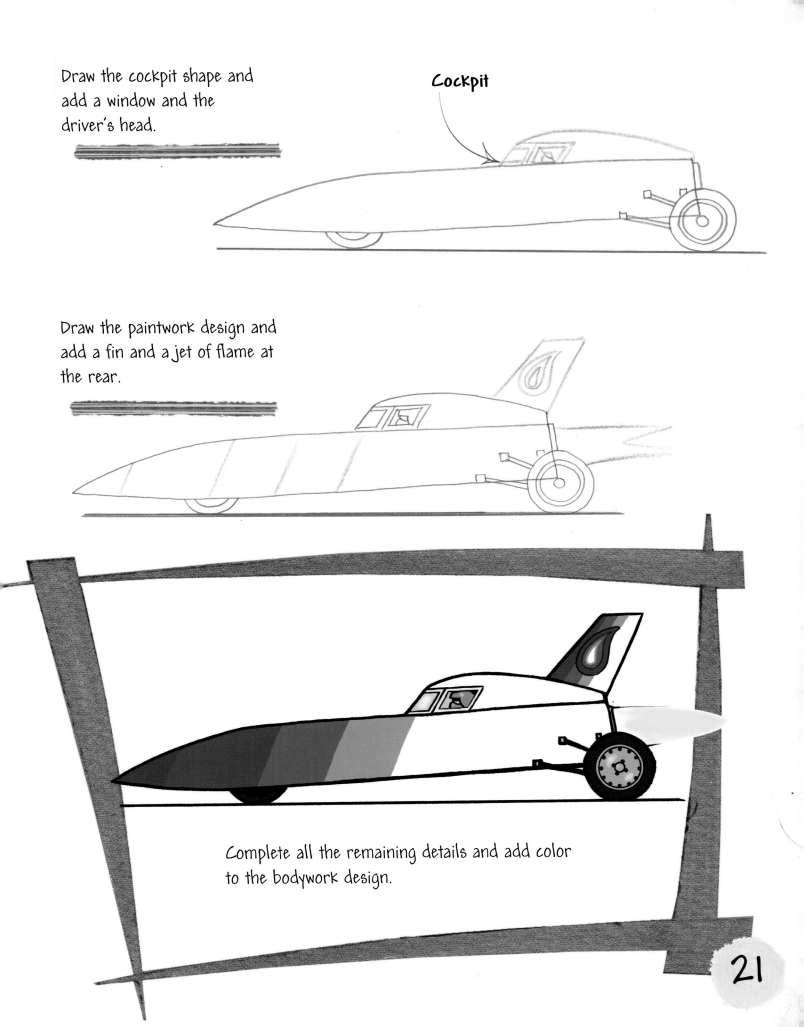

Complete all the remaining details and add color to the bodywork design.

Space shuttle

The space shuttle could carry astronauts and large payloads into space and then return to Earth to be used again.

Draw a rectangle for the main fuel tank. Add a long rectangle on each side of it for the Solid Rocket Boosters (SRBs)

Fuel Tank

SRB   **SRB**

Add a nose cone to each section, and add fairings and nozzles to the SRBs.

Nose cone

Fairings

Nozzle

Draw the main body of the shuttle.

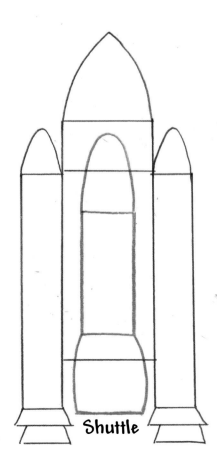

Shuttle

Draw the shuttle's wings and tail fin.

Add extra details to the SRBs. Draw the shuttle's windows and engine nozzles. Add three jets of flame.

Add any remaining details to finish off your shuttle, and then color the different sections.

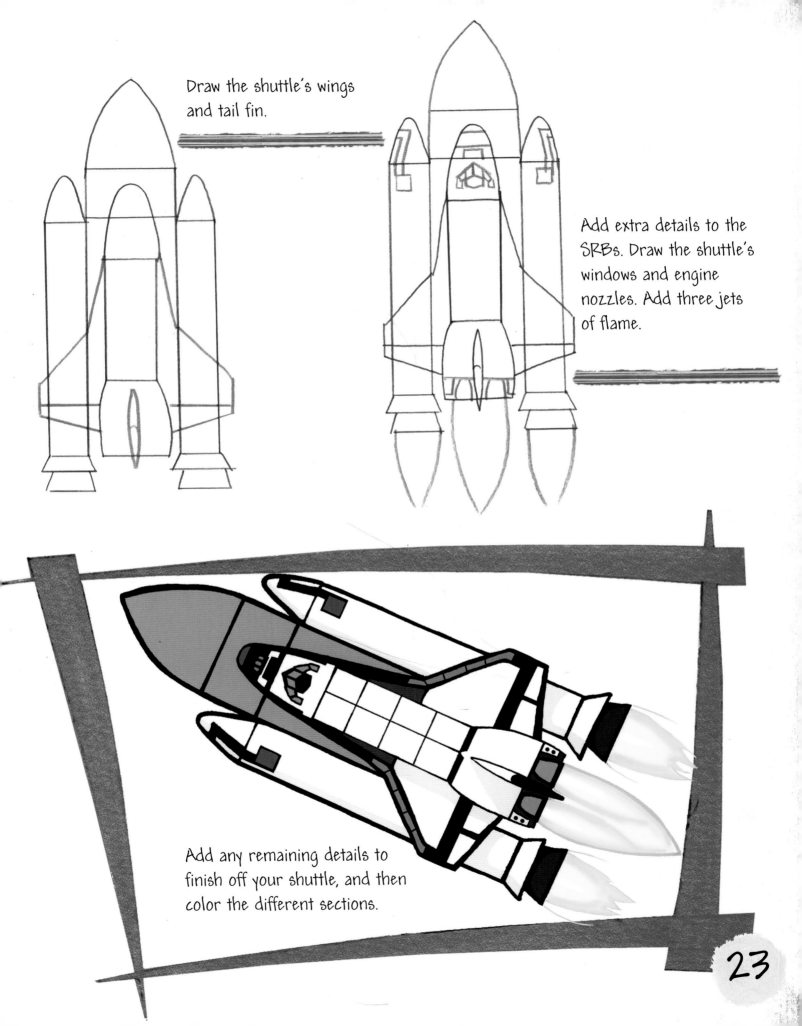

X-15

The X-15 is a high-speed experimental aircraft. It holds the world's speed record for a manned rocket-powered aircraft, reaching a speed of 4,519.966 mph (7,272.626 kph)!

Draw the main bullet-shaped fuselage.

Add the cockpit and the tail fin.

Cockpit

Tail fin

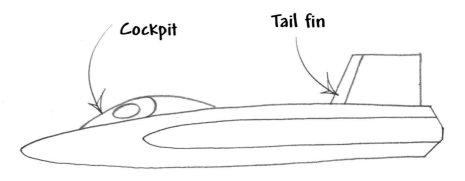

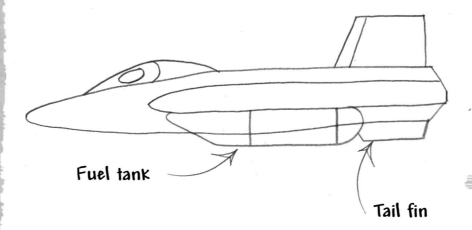

Fuel tank

Tail fin

Draw the auxiliary fuel tanks and the rear bottom tail fin.

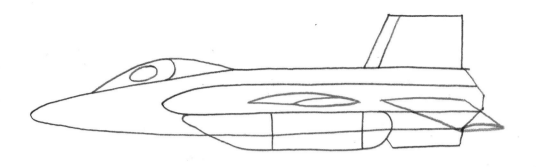

Draw a wing and rear
horizontal stabilizers.

Add all remaining
details to the X-15.

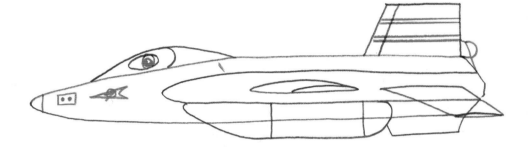

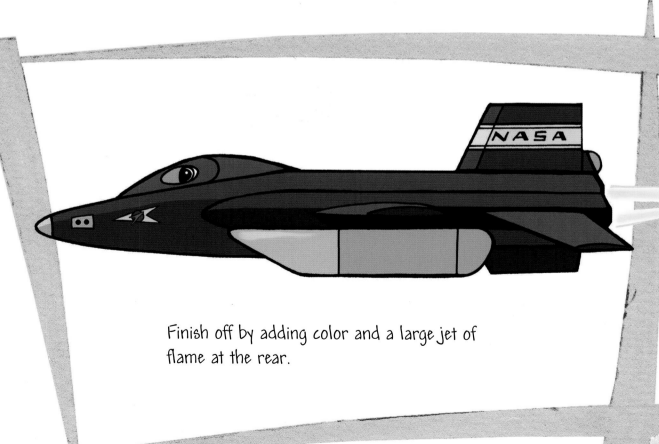

Finish off by adding color and a large jet of
flame at the rear.

Ariane

The Ariane rocket was developed in Europe in the 1970s. It is capable of carrying large payloads, such as satellites, into orbit.

Draw a tall rectangle for the main body of the rocket.

Add a nose cone to the top and a nozzle to the bottom.

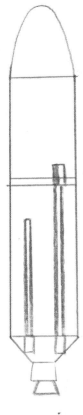

Add some detail to the main rocket sections.

Add a rectangle on either side of the rocket body for the SRBs.

SRB

SRB

Add a nose cone and other small details to each SRB. Draw the SRB fairings and nozzles, then add jets of flame.

Complete any remaining details and add color.

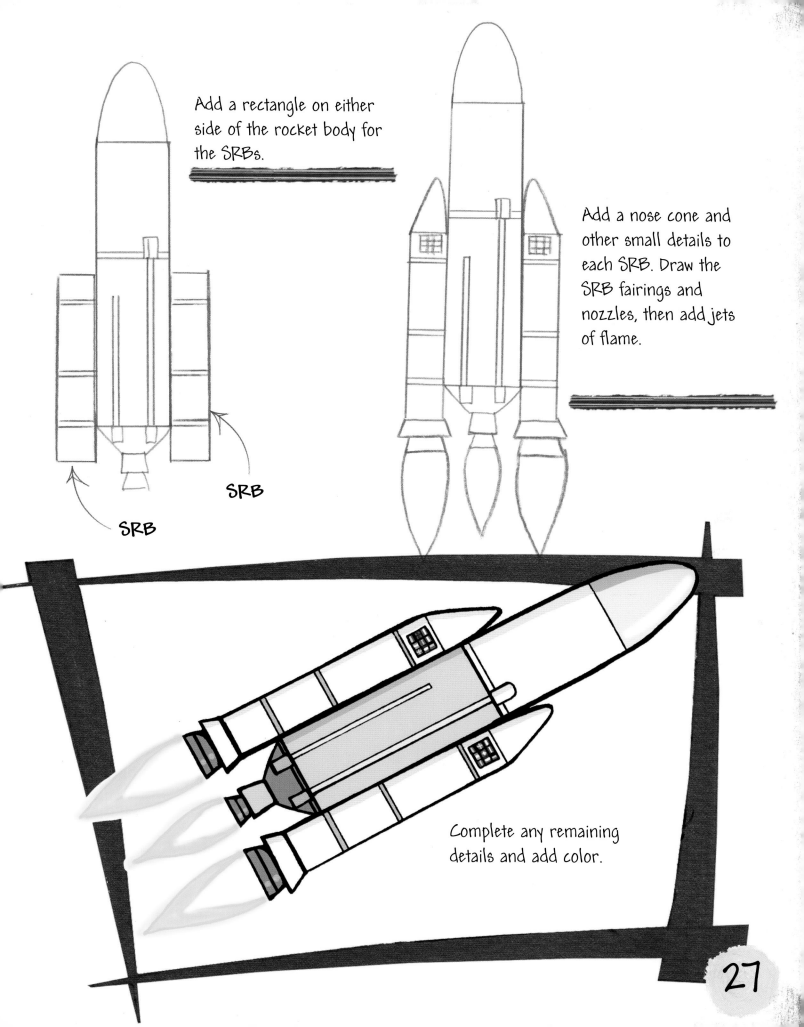

SpaceShipOne

SpaceShipOne completed the first ever manned tourist spaceflight in 2004.

Start by drawing the main body shape with an overlapping wing structure.

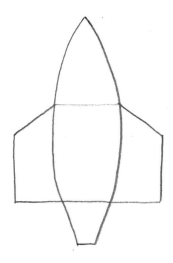

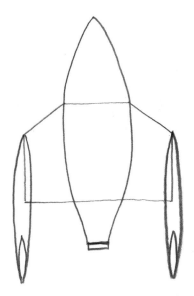

Add long extensions to each wing.

Add detail to the wings.

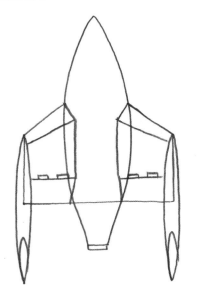

Windows

Draw the windows. Add a large jet of flame at the base.

Fins

Add fins to the wing structure.

Finish off by adding color and perhaps adding a design.

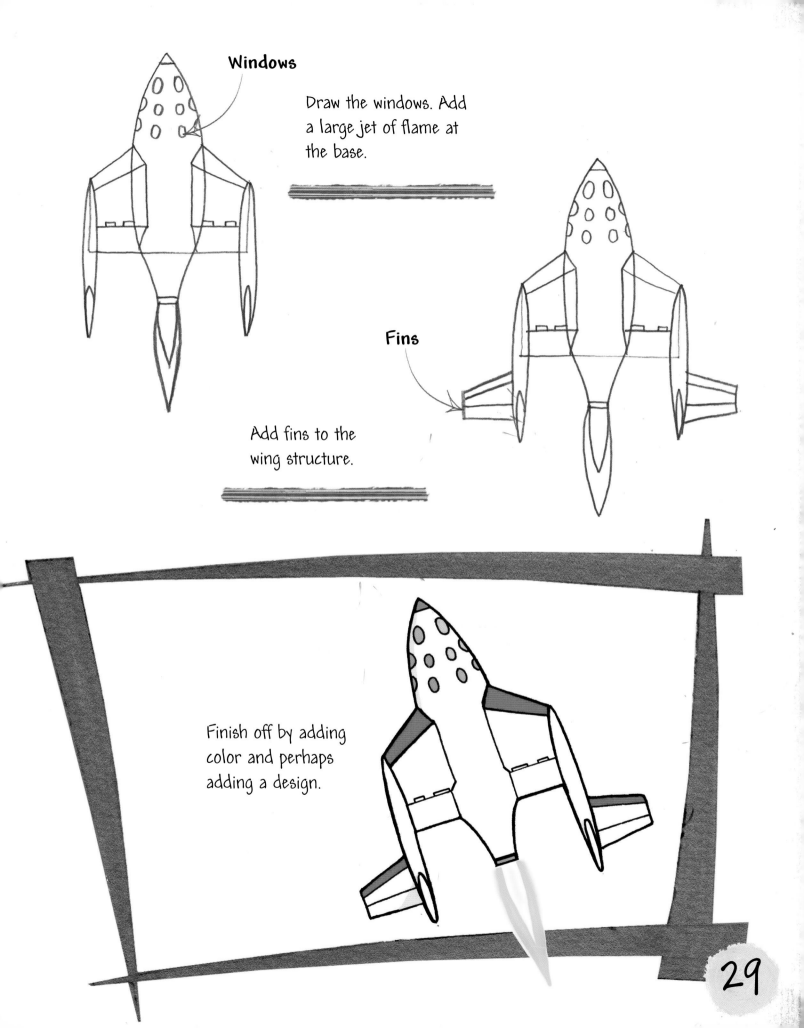

More views

For an extra challenge, try drawing rockets from the front or rear! Practicing different views will help you improve your drawing.

Back view

Start by drawing a large circle with two smaller circles on either side of it.

Draw in the shape of the space shuttle and add more details to the rocket nozzles.

Add the shuttle's wings and tail fin and join it to the fuel tank.

Add the small details to finish off. A pencil has been used to draw this example. Try other materials to create a different look.

Space shuttle

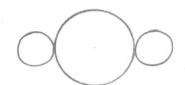

Shuttle

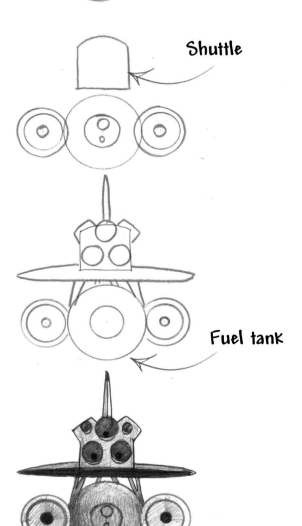

Fuel tank

Front view

Start by drawing
two circles, one
inside the other.

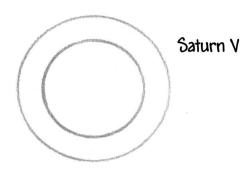

Saturn V

Add one more circle.

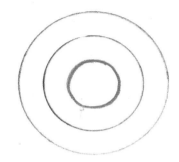

Draw the curved fairings,
the fins, and the square
escape tower. Start to
add the design.

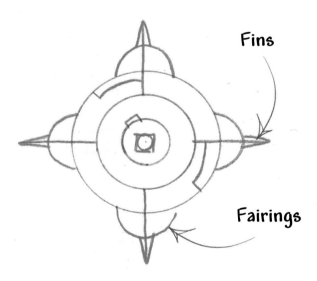

Fins

Fairings

Finish off this view of the
rocket by adding any
extra details. Now color
it if you want!

Glossary

auxiliary fuel tank A fuel tank that detaches from a rocket during a spaceflight.

command module The detachable portion of a spacecraft in which the astronauts live.

construction lines Guidelines used in the early stages of a drawing. They are usually erased later.

escape tower A tower connecting to an escape rocket, used in emergencies.

fairing A component that temporarily protects the payload of a spacecraft.

fuselage The main body of a spacecraft or aircraft.

payload The cargo of an aircraft or spacecraft, which could include extra fuel or scientific equipment.

rocket nozzle A component that increases the power of fuel in the rocket.

satellite A machine that orbits Earth.

SRB (solid rocket booster) A component that provides a boost to the rocket to help it launch.

stabilizer A horizontal or vertical wing that helps to balance the spacecraft or vehicle.

suborbital flight A spaceflight that reaches space but doesn't go far enough to enter the planet's orbit.

supersonic Faster than the speed of sound.

Index

A
antenna 17
Apollo CSM 16, 17
Ariane 26, 27
astronaut 22

B
Bell X-2 18, 19
Blue Flame 20, 21

C
cockpit 18, 19, 21, 24
command module 15
construction lines 8

D
driver 21

E
eraser 8
escape tower 13, 15, 31

F
fairings 15, 22, 27, 31
fins 12, 15, 18, 19, 21, 23, 24, 29, 30, 31
fuselage 18, 24

M
Mercury-Redstone 12, 13
moon, the 16

N
NASA 12, 14

P
pastel 9
pen 8, 9
pencil 8, 9
pilot 19

R
rocket nozzle 13, 15, 17, 22, 23, 26, 27, 30

S
satellite 26
Saturn V 14, 15, 31
SpaceShipOne 28, 29

space shuttle 22, 23, 30
speed records 20, 24
SRB (solid rocket booster) 22, 23, 27
stabilizers 18, 20, 25

T
thrusters 17

X
X-15 24, 25